Rose Elliot's Book of Fruits

Rose Elliot is the author of several bestselling cookbooks, and is renowned for her practical and creative approach. She writes regularly for the *Vegetarian* and has contributed to national newspapers and magazines as well as broadcasting on radio and television. She is married and has three children.

D1081233

Other titles available in the series

Rose Elliot's Book of Breads
Rose Elliot's Book of Salads
Rose Elliot's Book of Vegetables

Rose Elliot's Book of

Fruits

Fontana Paperbacks

First published by Fontana Paperbacks 1983

Set in 10 on 11pt Linotron Plantin
Illustrations by Vana Haggerty
Made and printed in Great Britain by
William Collins Sons & Co. Ltd, Glasgow

Introduction

Who can resist the first strawberries of the season, the luscious raspberries and redcurrants in July and the first of the shiny English apples of the early autumn?

This book is about making the most of fruit, how to prepare and cook it to enjoy it at its best, with ideas for using the glut fruits in different ways to get as much variety as possible. I have concentrated particularly on the main use of fruits in puddings and desserts and have included favourite traditional recipes as well as some ideas of my own.

BASIC PREPARATION AND COOKING

Buy ripe, firm fruit; prepare quickly, cutting with a sharp stainless steel knife and use as soon as possible. Coat cut surfaces of fruit which you're going to serve raw with lemon or orange juice to prevent discoloration.

The method of cooking fruit most frequently used, and one which is suitable for almost all types, is poaching. To poach fruit, first make a sugar syrup. For 450-700 g (1-1½ lb) fruit you need 275 ml (½ pint) water (or other liquid such as wine or cider) and 75 g (3 oz) granulated sugar. Honey can be used instead of sugar if preferred but will add its own quite strong flavour. Put the sugar or honey and water into a heavy-based saucepan and heat gently until dissolved. Then turn up the heat and boil rapidly for 2 minutes. Put in the prepared fruit, bring back to the boil, then leave to simmer gently until the fruit feels tender when pierced with the point of a sharp knife.

It's important to give large fruits like whole or halved pears and peaches time to cook right through to the centre or they may discolour. Allow at least 20-30 minutes for whole pears and 15-20 minutes for the others.

The syrup can be flavoured with thin slices of lemon or orange peel, a cinnamon stick, vanilla pod or a few heads of fresh elderflowers: add when making the syrup and remove before serving the fruit. (The vanilla pod can be rinsed, dried and used several times.)

Let the fruits cool in the syrup, or remove with a draining spoon and thicken the syrup by boiling rapidly until reduced in quantity.

Soft, juicy fruits are best poached in the minimum of water, or none at all. Put red and black currants, bilberries, cranberries and blackberries into a heavy-based saucepan with 2 tablespoons of water to 450-700 g (1-1½ lb) fruit and heat gently until the juices run and the fruit is tender. Instead of the water use butter for apples, redcurrant jelly for rhubarb. When fruit is soft, add sugar to taste: do not put this in sooner or the outside of the fruits may toughen.

Cooked fruit, as well as uncooked soft fruits such as raspberries and strawberries, can be puréed. Simply push through a sieve or mouli légumes, or, to make it easier, liquidize first then sieve. Serve as a sauce or make into ice cream, fools and sorbets.

Apple Use dessert apples with or without the skin; slice, core and add to salads or fruit salad mixtures, or grate to make a real fruit muesli (page 20). Stew apples as described on page 15; serve with cream and shortbread biscuits or as a sauce with savoury dishes. Or top with meringue (page 50), make into a crumble (page 24), charlotte (page 15), or ice cream (page 51). For baked apples, wash and core one large cooking apple for each person, score round the middle with a pointed knife to prevent the apple from bursting. Put the apples into a shallow baking dish then fill the centres with brown sugar, dates, raisins or a mixture of honey and nuts. Bake at 180°C (350°F), gas mark 4, for about 45 minutes. For apple pie, see recipes on pages 25 and 26, using uncooked apples in place of the fruits given.

Apricot Ripe apricots are delicious raw; less perfect apricots are best cooked. Poach in a vanilla-flavoured sugar syrup or put into a casserole with 3 tablespoons sugar and 1-2 tablespoons water to 450 g (1 lb) apricots and bake for 30-60 minutes at 180°C (350°F), gas mark 4. Cooked apricots can be made into a crumble, topped with meringue, served on a crisp pastry base or puréed and made into fools, ices or sorbets.

Banana Top sliced banana with a dollop of yoghurt or fromage blanc and some maple syrup or runny honey and chopped nuts; or, for a treat, peel and cut lengthwise, put a scoop of vanilla ice cream between the halves, top with chocolate sauce (page 45), and chopped nuts. Also good cooked in a crumble (page 24), or as banana beauharnais (page 23). Or make a slit down the top of a banana and bake whole in the oven, 190°C (375°F), gas mark 5, for about 20 minutes until soft, then serve with cream, yoghurt or rum butter.

Bilberry Known as blueberry in the USA, can be eaten raw with sugar and cream if very ripe and soft, but is usually best cooked. Wash and pick over the berries, make into a pie (page 25) or stew as described on page 15.

Blackberry Wash, pick over and serve with sugar and cream; or stew as described on page 15 and eat with cream or yoghurt, topped with crumble (page 24), or puréed and made into sorbets, sauces and fools. For blackberry ice cream follow the recipe on page 51 using cooked blackberries instead of raspberries.

Blackcurrant Wash and remove the stems or, for a purée leave the stems on. Stew as described on page 15. Blackcurrant purée is delicious with ice cream or made into a sorbet (page 29). Blackcurrants also make an excellent plate pie: (page 25).

Cherry Wash sweet cherries and serve them as they are, or remove stalks and stones and add to a fruit salad. Also delicious made into a compôte (page 28).

Cranberry Wash, remove damaged berries and small stems. To make a cranberry sauce cook as described on page 29. The sauce can be puréed and flavoured with red wine and grated orange rind. Cranberries also make a good tart: (page 30).

Date Shiny plump fresh dates can quite often be found at good

8

supermarkets and greengrocers now and are delicious. Serve as they are or slice and stone and add to fruit salads; or remove the stones and fill the centres with nuts or marzipan.

Fig Serve ripe figs Greek-style with a bowl of thick creamy yoghurt and runny honey, or slice and add to fruit salads.

Gooseberry Wash and leave as they are if you're going to purée them, otherwise 'top and tail', then cook in a sugar syrup as described on page 18. Add a few sprigs of elderflowers for a delicious muscat flavour. Can be puréed and made into a fool (page 34), or a sauce which is a traditional accompaniment for mackerel. Also make excellent pies: follow recipes on pages 25 and 26.

Grape Just wash gently and arrange in a fruit bowl or on a cheeseboard; or halve, remove seeds and add grapes to a fruit salad or arrange on top of a sponge cake and glaze with jam (page 35).

Grapefruit Halve across, loosen sections with a sharp knife, carefully ease out white skin and membranes. Can be sprinkled with sherry and a little sugar or topped with brown sugar and dots of butter and grilled. Or cut out the segments as described for oranges (page 40).

Greengage Prepare as for plums.

Kiwi fruit, Chinese gooseberry Should feel just soft to the touch. Use raw, peeled and sliced, in fruit salads and to decorate cheesecakes (page 36), fools and creams.

Lemon To use the skin, scrub well in warm water to remove residues of sprays, then grate finely, or pare off thinly. Use both the juice and the rind to flavour ice creams, fools and sorbets as well as cakes and pastries.

Lime Gives a delicious flavour to fools and creams and makes an unusual garnish for fruit fritters or pancakes.

Loganberry Prepare and use as for blackberries.

Lychee Looks like a small horsechestnut, with a reddish prickly shell. Inside is translucent white fragrant flesh and a large shiny brown stone. Serve raw, or peel, stone and add to an exotic fruit salad.

Mango Large oval fruits, green or gold, often splashed with red. They are ripe when soft to the touch. To prepare, first cut in half and remove the stone: make two downward cuts, each about 3 mm ($\frac{1}{8}$ in) from the stalk at the top. As you cut down you will feel the large flat stone, and the two halves will fall apart. Serve the halves as they are and scoop out the juicy golden flesh with a teaspoon; or cut off the skin, slice the mango and add to fruit salad. Mango also makes an excellent sorbet or ice cream (pages 49 and 51).

Melon *Cantaloupe melon* has a rough, wart-like skin and deep grooves, as if ready for slicing; the flesh is orange, fragrant and juicy. *Charantais melons* are smaller versions. *Musk melon* has a netted skin and green or yellow aromatic flesh; delicious little *ogen melons* belong to this group as do *winter melons* which have smooth green, yellow or white skins but very little flavour. *Honeydew melons* have ridged green or yellow skins and sweet white or pale green flesh. *Watermelons* have smooth green skin, scarlet flesh and shiny brown pips. Melons should feel heavy and yield to slight pressure at the stalk end. Serve large melons cut in slices, the smaller ones halved and maybe filled with sweet sherry or port, ripe strawberries or a scoop

10

of ice cream (page 38). They can also be made into a sorbet.

Nectarine Prepare as for peaches.

Orange Scrub skins, if using, to remove residue of sprays. Use the rind, either grated or thinly pared, for flavouring; the juice is good instead of sugar syrup in fruit salads. Oranges can be peeled and divided into segments; but the best way is to cut round and round with a sharp knife and a sawing action, removing both the peel and the white skin. Then insert the knife and cut each segment away from the inner skin. Hold the orange over a bowl to catch the juice. Good in fruit salad, or served on their own, as described on page 41.

Passion fruit *Granadilla* has a wrinkled brown skin, sweet fragrant greenish flesh and quite a number of seeds. Halve the fruits, scoop out the flesh and add to fruit salads or use to top ice cream.

Pawpaw Also called papaya and custard apple. Large pear-shaped fruits, green or greenish yellow. Smell fragrant and feel soft when ripe; flesh inside is pink with tiny black seeds. Halve, scoop out seeds and eat flesh with a teaspoon; or peel, slice and add to fruit salads.

Peach To skin peaches, put into a bowl, cover with boiling water and leave for 2 minutes; drain and slip off skins with a sharp knife. Slice and cover with sweet white wine, add to fruit salads or make into peach brulée (page 42).

Pear Wash thin-skinned dessert pears and serve simply, or peel, core and slice and serve with cream, a raspberry purée, or as part of a fruit salad. Both dessert and cooking pears are delicious poached, (page 45).

Persimmon Also called a sharon fruit, looks like a ripe tomato and is ready for eating when it feels very soft. Flesh is very sweet and tastes like fresh dates. Peel, slice and add to fruit salad.

Pineapple Should be dark golden brown in colour, have a pronounced sweet smell and feel slightly soft to the touch. Cut through the leafy top into wedges, cut off tough core, serve like melon as a starter; or halve small pineapples through the leafy top, scoop out the inside, dice, mix with strawberries and pile back into the skins and serve as a pudding, one half for each person. Also makes an excellent sorbet (page 49).

Plum Slice and stone sweet plums and add to fruit salad; poach sharper plums in syrup as described on page 50, make into pies (page 25), crumble (page 24) or meringue, (page 50).

Pomegranate Halve, scoop out the scarlet flesh, add to fruit salad or use as a topping for a pale creamy pudding or coleslaw.

Quince Peel, core and slice, then stew or add to pies. Makes an excellent jelly preserve. The fruits of the scarlet-flowered Japanese quince are edible and can be used in this way.

Raspberry Eat raw with cream and sugar, or make into ice cream (page 51), sorbet or a fresh purée for serving with ice cream or other fruits (page 43).

Redcurrant Prepare as described for blackcurrants; mix with raspberries and strawberries to make traditional dishes such as rødgrød from Denmark (page 54), summer pudding (page 58), or raspberry and redcurrant tart (page 52).

Rhubarb Cut off the leaves (don't eat, they're poisionous) and pull off any strings from the sides of the rhubarb. Cut rhubarb into even-sized pieces, stew as described on page 15; make into a fool (page 34), or crumble (page 24). Best not to serve rhubarb more than once a week because its high oxalic content prevents the absorption of magnesium and calcium.

Strawberry Wash gently, remove stems and serve strawberries with sugar and cream; or, French-style, with little cream cheese hearts (page 55), or in little sweet pastry tartlets with a glaze of red jam. For strawberries cardinal, hull and slice the strawberries and cover with a raspberry sauce (page 43).

Tangerine, satsuma, clementine and mandarin Peel and eat as they are, or divide into segments and add to fruit salads.

Apple Charlotte

I like to use a wide, shallow dish for this traditional pudding so that there is plenty of crisp topping to go with the soft buttery apples.

SERVES 4

700 g (1½ lb) cooking apples,
    peeled, cored and sliced
25 g (1 oz) sugar
125 g (4 oz) butter

6-8 thin slices of wholewheat
    bread, crusts removed
demerara sugar
powdered cinnamon

Put apples, sugar and 25 g (1 oz) butter into a heavy-based saucepan and cook gently until pulpy. Then beat with a wooden spoon until smooth.

Set oven to 200°C (400°F), gas mark 6. Melt the remaining butter. Dip both sides of the slices of bread in the melted butter, arrange on base and sides of a shallow ovenproof dish. Spoon apple mixture on top of the bread, cover with more buttery bread. Sprinkle with demerara sugar and cinnamon. Bake for about 40 minutes, until top is browned and crisp.

Eve's Pudding with a Lemon Topping

This variation of a traditional apple pudding produces a very light sponge on top of soft apples which become bathed in a lemon sauce during the cooking process.

SERVES 4

450 g (1 lb) cooking apples, peeled, cored and sliced

50 g (2 oz) caster sugar

For the sponge topping

125 g (4 oz) self-raising flour
1 teaspoon baking powder
125 g (4 oz) polyunsaturated margarine

125 g (4 oz) caster sugar
grated rind of 1 lemon
1 egg
3 tablespoons milk

Set oven to 180°C (350°F), gas mark 4. Lightly grease a 1 litre (1½ pint) pie dish. Put apples into pie dish; sprinkle with the 50 g (2 oz) sugar. Sift flour and baking powder into a bowl, add the margarine, sugar, lemon rind, egg and milk; beat until thoroughly combined. Spoon on top of apples, then bake for about 45 minutes, until fruit is soft and sponge springs back when touched lightly.

Apple Fritters

You can use either cooking or eating apples for these: cooking apples will form a purée inside the crisp batter while eating apples remain firm.

SERVES 4

2 medium-sized cooking apples
  or large eating apples

For the batter

125 g (4 oz) plain flour	oil for deep-frying
150 ml (5 fl oz) warm water	1 egg white, stiffly beaten
2 tablespoons oil or melted butter	icing sugar

First start the batter. Put flour, water and oil into a bowl and mix until smooth. Leave on one side. Heat oil to 190°C (375°F), or until it sizzles when a little batter is dropped into it. Peel and core apples, keeping them whole, then cut into 6 mm (¼ in) rounds. Fold egg white into batter. Dip apple slices in batter, coating well. Fry fritters for about 5 minutes making sure that the apple inside is tender when pierced. Drain on to kitchen paper; dust with icing sugar.

Apple and Honey Ice Cream
with Blackberry Sauce

This recipe combines two complementary flavours in an unusual way and the pale green ice looks pretty with the vivid deep red sauce.

SERVES 4

225 g (8 oz) cooking apples, peeled, cored and sliced

3 tablespoons clear honey

300 ml (10 fl oz) whipping cream, whipped

1 tablespoon grated lemon rind

For the sauce

225 g (8 oz) blackberries

1 tablespoon sugar

Put apples and honey into a heavy-based saucepan and cook gently until pulpy. Then liquidize and cool. Fold cream and lemon rind into cooled purée. Pour into suitable container and freeze until firm, beating once or twice during freezing. To make sauce, put blackberries into a heavy-based saucepan, cook gently for 10 minutes until pulpy, then add sugar, liquidize and sieve. Chill.

   Remove ice cream from freezer 30 minutes before serving; spoon into individual glasses and pour sauce on top.

Apple Muesli with Honey and Almonds

Muesli was originally devised by Dr Bircher-Benner as a way of getting patients at his clinic in Zurich to eat fruit. It would be served as a supper dish, with thin wholewheat bread and butter and herb tea. Now, since the arrival of the packet varieties, most people associate muesli with breakfast, though I usually serve this fruity version as a pudding.

SERVES 4

4 large sweet apples
150 ml (5 fl oz) natural yoghurt or
   fromage blanc
125 g (4 oz) rolled oats
1 tablespoon clear honey

1 tablespoon grated orange rind
25-50 g (1-2 oz) raisins
75 g (3 oz) flaked almonds,
   toasted under a moderate grill

Halve and core the apples, then grate them fairly coarsely. There's no need to peel them unless the skin is tough. Put the grated apple into a large bowl and stir in the yoghurt or fromage blanc, oats, honey, orange rind and raisins. Stir well, then divide between four bowls. Just before serving, sprinkle with the toasted almonds.

Apple and Raisin Compôte
with Orange

I am particularly fond of this compôte because it relies on the natural sweetness of the apples and raisins without added sugar. It's at its best and most luscious when made with Cox or other sweet apples, though it also works well with cooking apples, and they're what I normally use.

SERVES 4-6

900 g (2 lb) apples
25 g (1 oz) butter

225 g (8 oz) raisins
juice and grated rind of 1 orange

Peel, core and slice the apples, then put them into a heavy-based saucepan with the butter, raisins and orange juice and rind. Cook gently, with a lid on the pan, for about 10 minutes, stirring frequently, until the apples look pulpy. Serve hot or cold – I like it best cold – with fromage blanc or whipped cream. Some crunchy shortbread biscuits go well with it.

Open Apple Tart

This is mouthwatering with its topping of glazed apple slices, moist filling of apple purée and crisp pastry base.

SERVES 4-6

20 cm (8 in) pastry flan case,
    baked as on page 52

For the filling

900 g (2 lb) cooking apples,
    peeled, cored and sliced
25 g (1 oz) butter
75 g (3 oz) sugar

2 large Cox apples
3 tablespoons warmed sieved
    apricot jam

Put the cooking apples, butter and sugar into a heavy-based saucepan and cook gently, uncovered, for about 15 minutes. The mixture should be able to hold its shape, so if necessary turn up heat and cook until this stage is reached, stirring often. Cool. Set the oven to 200°C (400°F), gas mark 6. Spoon apple purée into flan case. Peel Cox apples and slice thinly, arrange on top of purée, then spoon the jam over them. Bake for 20-30 minutes, until the apple slices are tender. Serve warm or cold.

Bananas Beauharnais

Beauharnais was the surname of Napoleon's first wife who came from the Caribbean and introduced this dish. It makes a delicious quick pudding.

SERVES 4

4 bananas
25 g (1 oz) butter
50 g (2 oz) soft brown sugar
4 tablespoons white rum

whipped cream
a few ratafias or 1-2 macaroons,
    crushed

Heat the grill to moderate; peel the bananas. Melt the butter in a shallow flameproof dish and put in the bananas and sugar. Fry the bananas gently in the butter for about 5 minutes, until beginning to soften. Then sprinkle with the sugar and rum and place under the grill for about 5 minutes until the sugar melts and bubbles. Serve at once, topped with cream and sprinkled with crushed ratafias or macaroons.

Banana Crumble

Quite an unusual way to treat bananas, but one of my favourites, and it's fast and easy to make. Serve with cream, fromage blanc or natural yoghurt.

SERVES 4

4 bananas	25 g (1 oz) butter
125 g (4 oz) wholewheat flour	50 g (2 oz) soft brown sugar
50 g (2 oz) ground almonds	25 g (1 oz) flaked almonds

Set the oven to 190°C (375°F), gas mark 5. Peel and slice the bananas and arrange them in a lightly greased, shallow, ovenproof dish. Put the flour and ground almonds into a bowl and mix in the butter, using a fork: the mixture should look like breadcrumbs. Add the sugar and flaked almonds and scatter over the top of the bananas. Bake in the oven for about 20 minutes.

Bilberry Plate Pie

I use wholewheat flour as I like its flavour and wholesome appearance, but white flour or a half-and-half mixture could be used instead.

SERVES 4-6

For the pastry

225 g (8 oz) plain wholewheat
   flour
125 g (4 oz) soft margarine

25 g (1 oz) caster sugar
3 tablespoons cold water
milk to glaze

For the filling

450 g (1 lb) bilberries, stalks
   removed

50 g (2 oz) sugar
15 g (½ oz) butter

Set oven to 200°C (400°F), gas mark 6. Sift flour into a bowl, adding bran from sieve. Rub in the margarine, add sugar and water, mix to a dough. Roll out a third of pastry, use to line a 20-22 cm (8-9 in) pie plate. Put bilberries on top, sprinkle with sugar, dot with butter. Roll out rest of pastry and put over top of fruit. Trim, decorate, and make two or three steam holes. Brush with milk. Bake for about 30 minutes.

Deep-dish Blackberry and Apple Pie

SERVES 4-6

For the pastry

225 g (8 oz) wholewheat flour
2 teaspoons baking powder
50 g (2 oz) butter

50 g (2 oz) white vegetable fat
3 tablespoons cold water

For the filling

450 g (1 lb) blackberries, washed
450 g (1 lb) apples, peeled, cored
  and sliced
75-100 g (3-4 oz) sugar

2-3 tablespoons water
milk to glaze
caster sugar

Set oven to 200°C (400°F), gas mark 6. Make pastry as in previous recipe, roll out quite thickly, and cut out so that it is about 2.5 cm (1 in) larger all round than pie dish. Cut 1 cm (½ in) strips of pastry from trimmings, brush with cold water, press round rim of pie dish. Mix fruit with sugar and put in dish; sprinkle with water. Ease pastry on top of fruit, moulding it over. Trim, decorate, and make steam holes. Brush with milk, bake for 15 minutes, then reduce the heat to 180°C (350°F), gas mark 4, for 15-20 minutes. Sprinkle with caster sugar.

Black Cherry Compôte

If you have the patience to stone the cherries, this makes a delicious summer pudding; it also works well using frozen (ready stoned) cherries.

SERVES 4

1 kg (2¼ lb) sweet black cherries
150 ml (¼ pint) red wine
2 tablespoons sugar

whipped cream or fromage blanc
to serve

Wash the fruit and remove stalks. Then use a cherry stoner to remove the stones. Put the wine and sugar into a heavy-based saucepan and heat gently until the sugar has dissolved, then boil for 2 minutes. Add the fruit and cook gently, covered with a lid, for 10-15 minutes, until the cherries are tender. Cool, then pour the mixture into a glass bowl and chill before serving. It's delicious with lightly whipped cream and the crunchy almond biscuits on page 44.

Blackcurrant Sorbet
with Cassis

This is also good made with bottled blackcurrants; you need two 375 g (13 oz) bottles in place of the fresh blackcurrants, water and sugar.

SERVES 4-6

450 g (1 lb) fresh blackcurrants,
    washed
150 ml (¼ pint) water
125 g (4 oz) sugar

1 egg white
6 tablespoons cassis
a little lightly whipped cream
    (optional)

Put the blackcurrants and water into a saucepan, cook gently for 10-15 minutes until soft, then add sugar. Liquidize, then sieve. (If you're using bottled blackcurrants, just liquidize and sieve them.) Reserve 3 tablespoonfuls. Pour the rest into suitable container and freeze until solid round edges. Whisk egg white until stiff, add the frozen blackcurrant purée, still whisking, to make a fluffy mixture. Pour back into container and freeze again until solid. Make a simple sauce by mixing reserved purée with the cassis.

Take the sorbet out of fridge 30 minutes before eating. Serve in individual glasses with sauce on top and cream if liked.

Cranberry Lattice Tart
with Orange Pastry

I wanted to use cranberries for something other than a sauce, and this tart was the result. The combination of crisp orange-flavoured pastry, sharp, slightly bitter cranberries and crunchy sugar works well.

SERVES 4

For the pastry

225 g (8 oz) plain flour
125 g (4 oz) butter
25 g (1 oz) sugar

grated rind of 1 orange and 3 tablespoons juice

For the filling

175 g (6 oz) fresh cranberries
75 g (3 oz) caster sugar

2 tablespoons water
extra caster sugar

Set oven to 200°C (400°F), gas mark 6. Make pastry as on page 25, adding orange rind and the juice instead of water. Roll out and use to line a 20 cm (8 in) shallow flan tin. Trim edges. Put cranberries on top of pastry and sprinkle with sugar and water. Re-roll trimmings, cut into strips and arrange in a lattice across on top of cranberries. Bake for 30 minutes, sprinkle with sugar and serve warm or cold.

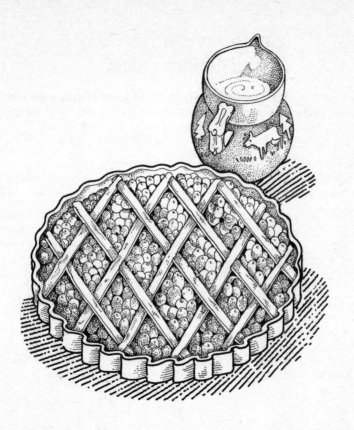

Exotic Fruit Salad

In this fruit salad, fresh orange juice is used instead of sugar syrup for a lighter, fresher result.

SERVES 4-6

1 small ripe pineapple
1 ripe mango
4 kiwi fruit

1 pawpaw
150 ml (¼ pint) orange juice

Cut the leafy top and prickly skin from the pineapple and remove the 'eyes' with a sharp pointed knife. Cut the pineapple into even-sized pieces and put into a bowl. Halve the mango and remove the stone and peel. Cut the flesh into dice and add to the bowl. Peel and slice the kiwi fruit, peel, de-seed and slice the pawpaw. Add these to the bowl, together with the orange juice. Chill before serving.

Gooseberry Fool with Pistachio Nuts and Crystallized Rose Petals

The bright green pistachio nuts and rose petals look very pretty against the pale green velvety fool, but of course these can be left off or replaced by chopped toasted almonds or hazel nuts if you prefer.

SERVES 6

900 g (2 lb) gooseberries
275 ml (½ pint) water
50-125 g (2-4 oz) sugar or honey
275 ml (10 fl oz) whipping cream,
    whipped, or fromage blanc

shelled pistachio nuts and
    crystallized rose petals

Put gooseberries into a saucepan with the water (no need to top and tail them) and simmer gently for about 10 minutes, until soft. Drain, reserving liquid. Liquidize then sieve gooseberries, adding some cooking liquid if necessary to make up to 475 ml (1 pint). Add sugar or honey to taste. Cool. Fold cream or fromage blanc lightly into the gooseberry purée. Spoon mixture into 6 glasses or one serving bowl. Decorate with chopped green pistachio nuts and crystallized rose petals.

Grape Sponge with Apricot Glaze

A light sponge topped with circles of grapes and a shiny apricot glaze.

SERVES 6

For the sponge base

100 g (3½ oz) self-raising flour: I use 81 per cent wholewheat

1 teaspoon baking powder

100 g (3½ oz) caster sugar

100 g (3½ oz) soft margarine

2 eggs

For the topping and glaze

125 g (4 oz) black grapes, halved and stoned

125 g (4 oz) green grapes, halved and stoned

4-5 rounded tablespoons sieved apricot jam, warmed

Set oven to 180°C (350°F), gas mark 4; grease a 20 cm (8 in) flan tin. Sift flour and baking powder into a bowl, add sugar, margarine and eggs and beat until light and fluffy. Spoon into flan tin and bake for 25-30 minutes. Cool. Brush some jam over sponge, arrange grapes in circles on top of jam, then spoon remaining jam over them. Serve with pouring cream.

Kiwi Fruit
and Lime Cheesecake

This is a cheesecake which makes the most of two green fruits: limes, which are used to flavour the cheesecake, and kiwi fruit which are arranged on top.

SERVES 8-10

75 g (3 oz) butter
175 g (6 oz) digestive biscuits,
    crushed
225 g (8 oz) curd cheese
grated rind and juice of 2 limes

50 g (2 oz) caster sugar
150 ml (5 fl oz) double cream
3 kiwi fruit, peeled and sliced
2 rounded tablespoons lime
    marmalade, warmed

Melt butter and mix with biscuit crumbs. Press into base and up sides of a 20 cm (8 in) loose-base flan tin and chill in fridge. Beat curd cheese, lime rind and juice and sugar until smooth. Whisk cream until stiff, add to the cheese mixture and beat well until mixture stands in soft peaks. Spoon into flan case; smooth top. Chill for at least 2 hours. Arrange kiwi fruits on top of cheesecake. Pour the marmalade over kiwi fruit. Cool, then remove from tin and serve.

Melon Filled with Ginger Ice Cream

SERVES 6

3 small ripe melons, preferably
  ogen, halved and de-seeded

For the ice cream

125 g (4 oz) granulated sugar
150 ml (¼ pint) water
3 eggs
300 ml (10 fl oz) whipping cream,
  whipped

6 pieces of stem ginger, chopped
a little syrup from the jar of
  ginger

Put sugar and water into a heavy-based saucepan and heat gently until dissolved. Turn up heat and boil steadily for about 5 minutes until the syrup thickens and will form a thread between your finger and thumb. Keep testing, removing the pan from the heat as you do so. Meanwhile put eggs into a bowl and whisk until light and frothy. Pour sugar syrup over beaten eggs, whisking all the time, until mixture is very light and pale. Cool, then fold in cream and ginger. Pour into container and freeze until solid, beating once. Serve melons with a scoop of ice cream in the centre and a spoonful of ginger syrup on top.

Fresh Orange Salad with Honey and Orange Flower Water

One of the most refreshing puddings I know, this is delicious served well-chilled. The orange flower water is optional; it can be bought at chemists and gives a fragrant, honeyed flavour to this dish.

SERVES 4-6

1 tablespoon honey, preferably
    orange blossom
2 tablespoons boiling water
6 large oranges

150 ml (¼ pint) orange juice
2 tablespoons orange flower
    water: optional

Put the honey into a large bowl and mix with the boiling water until dissolved. Scrub one of the oranges in warm water and pare off the peel with a potato peeler. Cut the peel into fine shreds and add to the honey and water. Then cut the peel and pith from the oranges, holding them over the bowl as you do so to catch any juice. Cut the segments away from the inner skin and put them into the bowl. Squeeze the remaining skin over the bowl to extract any extra juice. Add the 150 ml (¼ pint) orange juice to the oranges in the bowl, together with the orange flower water. Stir well, then chill before serving.

Orange Water Ice
Served in Orange Skins

This makes an attractive pudding and once assembled it can be stored in the freezer until just before you want to eat it.

SERVES 4

275 ml (½ pint) water
125 g (4 oz) sugar
4 large oranges

juice of half a lemon
extra orange juice: see recipe
2 egg whites

Put water and sugar into a heavy-based saucepan and heat gently until sugar has dissolved; then simmer gently for 10 minutes. Cool. Slice tops off oranges and scoop out the flesh, keeping skins whole. Liquidize then sieve orange flesh, add lemon juice and extra orange juice if necessary to make 275 ml (½ pint). Add this to the cooled syrup, then pour mixture into suitable container and freeze until solid round the edges. Whisk the egg whites until stiff, then beat in orange mixture. Freeze until firm, then spoon into the orange skins and put back tops as 'lids'. Wrap oranges in clingfilm and freeze until 15 minutes before eating.

Peach Brulée

One of my favourite fruit dishes and always popular for a dinner party, yet very quick and simple to prepare, and convenient because it is best made in advance. You can make a healthier, slimmer's version by replacing the whipped cream with fromage blanc or using half cream and half fromage blanc.

SERVES 6

6 large ripe peaches
2-3 tablespoons orange, peach or apricot liqueur: optional

275 ml (10 fl oz) double cream or fromage blanc
demerara sugar

Put the peaches into a bowl and cover with boiling water. Leave for 2 minutes, then drain the peaches and slip off the skins with a sharp pointed knife. Halve, stone and thinly slice the peaches. Put the slices into a shallow dish that's suitable for putting under the grill. Sprinkle with the liqueur if you're using it. Whip the cream until it stands in soft peaks, then spoon this on top of the peaches, smoothing it evenly over them. Cover with an even layer of demerara sugar. Heat the grill to moderate; put the peach mixture under the grill until the sugar melts. Remove from the heat; cool, then chill for several hours before serving.

Peaches Cardinal

A simple, very effective dish: halved peaches bathed in raspberry purée, the colour of a cardinal's robe.

SERVES 4

350 g (12 oz) fresh or frozen
   raspberries
25-50 g (1-2 oz) icing sugar or
   clear honey

4 ripe peaches

First make the raspberry purée sauce. Sieve or (and I think this is easier) liquidize then sieve the raspberries. Stir in enough icing sugar or honey to sweeten. Put the peaches into a bowl, cover with boiling water and leave for 2 minutes. Then drain and slip off the skins with a sharp knife. Halve the peaches and remove stones. Lay the peaches, rounded side up, in a shallow serving dish and pour the raspberry purée on top. Chill before serving.

Peaches in White Wine with Crisp Almond Tuiles

SERVES 6

6 ripe peaches	a little sugar to taste
275 ml (½ pint) sweet white wine	

For the almond tuile biscuits

75 g (3 oz) butter	50 g (2 oz) plain flour
75 g (3 oz) caster sugar	50 g (2 oz) flaked almonds
a few drops almond essence	

Cover peaches with boiling water for 2 minutes, then skin. Halve, stone and thinly slice peaches. Put into a glass bowl and cover with wine. Add sugar to taste. Chill.

To make biscuits, set oven to 200°C (400°F), gas mark 6. Beat butter and sugar until light, stir in essence, flour and almonds. Put teaspoonfuls on to a greased baking sheet and flatten with a fork, allowing plenty of room to spread. Bake until browned at the edges: 6-8 minutes. Leave to stand for 1-2 minutes until firm enough to lift from tin, but not brittle, then place over a rolling pin to curl as they cool. Serve with the peaches.

Pears Belle Hélène

This rich classic fruit dish is wonderful for a special treat.

SERVES 4

For the pears
275 ml (½ pint) water
3 tablespoons granulated sugar
1 vanilla pod

4 large pears, peeled, halved
and cored

For the sauce
125 g (4 oz) plain chocolate
2 tablespoons water
vanilla ice cream made as
described on page 38, omitting

ginger and adding ½ teaspoon
vanilla essence: or use good
quality bought ice cream

Make a sugar syrup from the water and sugar as described on page 29.
Poach pears gently in the syrup for at least 10 minutes until tender.
Cool. Just before serving, make the sauce: break chocolate into a
bowl, add water and set over a pan of steaming water until the
chocolate has melted; stir gently. Put a portion of ice cream in each
dish between two pear halves, and top with chocolate sauce.

Pear Tart with Chocolate Pastry

SERVES 4-6

For the pastry
175 g (5 oz) plain flour
25 g (1 oz) cocoa powder
125 g (4 oz) butter

50 g (2 oz) vanilla sugar or
   caster sugar
a few drops vanilla essence

For the filling
275 ml (½ pint) water
3 tablespoons sugar
1 vanilla pod
3 large pears, peeled, halved
   and cored

150 ml (5 fl oz) whipping cream:
   optional

Bake a pastry flan case as on page 52, sifting the cocoa with the flour.
(If during cooking the pastry slides down the tin, gently press it back
against the base and sides, using a fork when flan is done.) Cool.
Prepare pears, as on page 45; remove from the syrup, cut into thin
slices and arrange, like the spokes of a wheel, in the flan. Boil syrup
until reduced to 2 tablespoons: spoon on top of pears. Serve as it is, or
with whipped cream.

Pears in Red Wine

These pears, cooked whole and deeply stained by the red wine, make a most attractive pudding. Serve them with whipped cream that's been lightly flavoured with cinnamon and the almond biscuits on page 44.

SERVES 6

125 g (4 oz) sugar
275 ml (½ pint) water
275 ml (½ pint) red wine

6 ripe pears
whipped cream flavoured with a
   little sugar and cinnamon

Put the sugar, water and wine into a heavy-based saucepan and heat gently until the sugar has dissolved. Then boil rapidly for 2 minutes. Peel the pears, keeping them whole and leaving the stalks on. Put them into the syrup and let them cook gently, with a lid on the pan, for 30 minutes (or longer if necessary) until they are really tender. Remove the pears to a shallow serving dish. Thicken the cooking liquid if necessary by boiling rapidly without a lid until reduced to 3-4 tablespoons; spoon over the pears.

Pineapple Sorbet

Here, a pineapple is halved and the flesh made into a sorbet, served in the skins and decorated with fresh strawberries.

SERVES 6

1 large ripe pineapple
125 g (4 oz) granulated sugar
475 ml (1 pint) water

1 egg white
225 g (8 oz) small, ripe
   strawberries

Halve the pineapple from top to bottom, cutting right through the leaves. Scoop out flesh, discarding hard core. Heat sugar and water gently in a pan until sugar has dissolved, then boil for 2 minutes. Liquidize pineapple with this sugar syrup. Put the mixture into a shallow container and freeze until solid around the edges. Whisk egg white, then add pineapple mixture, and whisk until well blended. Freeze mixture until solid. About 30 minutes before you want to eat the sorbet take it out of the fridge. Spoon the sorbet into the pineapple skins and decorate with strawberries.

Plum Meringue

I like to bake this in quite a cool oven so that the meringue gets crisp, contrasting well with the soft, slightly sharp plums beneath.

SERVES 4

900 g (2 lb) plums, halved and stoned

50 g (2 oz) sugar

For the meringue
2 egg whites

125 g (4 oz) caster sugar

Put plums into a heavy-based saucepan and heat gently until the juices run. If the plums look as though they are going to burn, add a few tablespoons water. Cover the pan and leave to cook gently until the plums are tender, 15-30 minutes, depending on the type and ripeness of the plums, then stir in the sugar. Spoon the mixture into a shallow heatproof dish. Set the oven to 150°C (300°F), gas mark 2. Whisk the egg whites until very stiff, then add half the sugar and beat until glossy. Fold in the remaining sugar with a metal spoon. Spread this mixture gently on top of the plums, making sure that the meringue reaches to the edges of the dish. Bake for 1-1½ hours until the meringue is crisp and lightly browned.

Raspberry Ice Cream

Other berry fruits such as strawberries, blackberries or loganberries can be used for this ice cream, which is a very easy one to make.

SERVES 4-6

350 g (12 oz) fresh or frozen raspberries	125 g (4 oz) icing sugar
	275 ml (10 fl oz) whipping cream

Liquidize then sieve the raspberries. Add the icing sugar to the purée. Whip the cream until it's standing in soft peaks, then fold into the raspberry purée. Turn the mixture into a shallow polythene container and freeze until firm, beating once or twice during this process. Take it out of the freezer at the beginning of the meal to allow it to soften a little before serving.

Raspberry and Redcurrant Tart

A pretty, jewelled tart to make from ripe fruit at the height of summer.

SERVES 4-6

For the pastry

125 g (4 oz) plain flour

50 g (2 oz) butter

25 g (1 oz) caster sugar

1 egg yolk

For the filling

350 g (12 oz) raspberries

125 g (4 oz) redcurrants, washed and stems removed

225 g (8 oz) redcurrant jelly, warmed

Sift the flour into a bowl and rub in the butter until the mixture looks like breadcrumbs. Add sugar and egg yolk; mix to form a dough. Cover with polythene and chill for 30 minutes. Set the oven to 200°C (400°F), gas mark 6. Roll out pastry and line a 20 cm (8 in) flan tin with a removable base. Prick base, trim sides. Bake for 15 minutes. Cool. Arrange circles of raspberries and redcurrants in the flan. Pour redcurrant jelly over fruit; cool.

Rhubarb Crumble with Wholewheat Ginger Topping

Other flavourings can be used instead of ginger: cinnamon and grated orange rind are both good.

SERVES 4

900 g (2 lb) rhubarb

50 g (2 oz) caster or soft brown sugar

For the crumble topping
175 g (6 oz) self-raising wholewheat flour
1 teaspoon powdered ginger

125 g (4 oz) butter or margarine
125 g (4 oz) demerara sugar

Set the oven to 200°C (400°F), gas mark 6. Wash the rhubarb and cut off the leafy tops. Cut the stalks into even-sized chunks and place in a lightly greased, fairly shallow baking dish. Sprinkle with the caster or brown sugar. Next make the crumble. Sift the flour and ginger into a bowl, adding the residue of bran from the sieve. Rub in the butter or margarine with your finger tips until the mixture looks like breadcrumbs, then stir in the demerara sugar. Bake for about 30 minutes, until the crumble is crisp and the rhubarb underneath is tender when pierced with a sharp knife.

Rødgrød

This red fruit pudding from Denmark is delicious.

SERVES 6

450 g (1 lb) fresh ripe red fruit: raspberries, redcurrants, strawberries, or a mixture
125 g (4 oz) caster sugar

475 ml (1 pint) water
50 g (2 oz) cornflour or arrowroot
a little lemon juice
whipped cream to serve

Put the fruit into the liquidizer with the sugar and water and blend to a purée; sieve. Mix the cornflour or arrowroot to a paste with a little of this purée; put the rest into a saucepan and heat to boiling point. Pour the boiling purée over the cornflour or arrowroot paste, then return to the pan and stir until the mixture thickens. Taste and sharpen with a little lemon juice if necessary. Pour the mixture into 4 individual bowls and leave to cool. It looks pretty with some whipped cream on top and goes well with the almond biscuits on page 44.

Strawberry Tartlets

Delicious, fragile tartlets of early summer which melt in your mouth.
Serve them as they are, or with pouring cream.

SERVES 4

For the pastry
175 g (6 oz) plain flour
125 g (4 oz) butter

2 teaspoons caster sugar
1-2 tablespoons cold water

For the filling
4 rounded tablespoons
  redcurrant jelly, warmed

225 g (8 oz) small strawberries,
  hulled

Make pastry as on page 25; cover with polythene and chill for 30
minutes. Set the oven to 190°C (375°F), gas mark 5. Roll out pastry
and use a cutter to stamp out circles to fit small tartlets. Prick lightly,
bake for about 8 minutes, then cool. Brush a little redcurrant jelly
over each tartlet case, then arrange about three or four strawberries in
each and spoon some redcurrant jelly over them so that they glisten.
Cool before serving.

Strawberries with Coeurs à la Crème

You can buy the little white china moulds for these at kitchen shops, or you can use yoghurt pots with drainage holes in the base.

SERVES 5-6

450 g (1 lb) curd cheese
150 ml (5 fl oz) double cream
2 tablespoons caster sugar

350 g (12 oz) strawberries
a little extra caster sugar

Beat together the cheese, cream and sugar until very thick. Line 5 or 6 hearts or yoghurt pots with muslin, spoon in the cream mixture and smooth surface. Stand containers on a plate and chill overnight.

Just before you want to serve the dish, wash and hull the strawberries, halving or quartering any large ones so that they are all roughly the same size. Turn the white cheese mixture out on to one large plate or individual ones, arrange the strawberries round and sprinkle with caster sugar.

Summer Pudding

Although I use wholewheat bread for almost all my cooking, this is one occasion when I think you need to use white bread.

SERVES 4-6

700 g (1½ lb) red fruit;
    raspberries, redcurrants,
    blackcurrants and
    strawberries, as available

125 g (4 oz) caster sugar
8-10 thin slices of white bread,
    crusts removed

Wash the fruit and remove stems and stalks as necessary. Put the fruit into a large heavy-based saucepan with the sugar and heat gently until the sugar has dissolved and the juices are running. Remove from the heat. Lightly grease a 1 litre (2 pint) pudding basin. Soak pieces of bread in the juice from the fruit, then arrange in the pudding basin so that it is completely covered. Pour the fruit in on top of the bread and cover with more bread to make a lid. Place a plate and a weight on top and leave in a cool place for several hours, or overnight if possible. To serve, dip the basin in very hot water, slip a knife around the edge of the pudding, then invert over a plate. Serve with whipped cream.

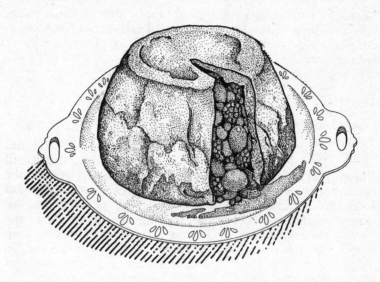

Winter Fruit Salad

Winter is, surprisingly, a very good time for making a fruit salad: excellent apples such as Cox and Russet are easy to come by and there are plenty of good citrus fruits, and grapes. This is a simple, refreshing salad, made with fruit juice instead of sugar syrup and is very good after you've eaten too many rich things at Christmas!

SERVES 4-6

2 large oranges	225 g (8 oz) black or green grapes
4 tangerines or similar	150 ml (¼ pint) orange juice
2 large apples, preferably Cox	

Cut the peel and pith off the oranges, cutting right into the flesh and holding them over a bowl to catch the juice. Then cut the segments away from the inner white skin. Put these into the bowl. Peel the tangerines and divide into segments; peel, core and slice the apples; wash, halve and de-seed the grapes. Add all these to the bowl, together with the orange juice, and mix well. Chill before serving.

Index

Apple(s) 7
  baked 7
  charlotte 15
  fritters 17
  and honey ice cream
    with blackberry sauce 18
  muesli with honey
    and almonds 20
  and raisin compôte
    with orange 21
  tart, open 22
Apricot(s) 7
  poached 7

Banana(s) 7-8
  Beauharnais 23
  crumble 24
Bilberry 8
  plate pie 25
Blackberry 8
  and apple pie, deep-dish 26
  sauce, apple and honey
    ice cream with 18

Black cherry
  compôte 28
Blackcurrant 8
  sorbet with cassis 29
Brulée, peach 42

Cardinal, peaches 43
Charlotte, apple 15
Cheesecake, kiwi
  fruit and lime 36
Cherry 8
  compôte, black 28
Chinese gooseberry 9
Clementine 13
Coeurs à la crême,
  strawberries with 57
Compôte
  apple and raisin, with
    orange 21
  black cherry 28
Cooking of fruit 5-6
Cranberry 8
  lattice tart with orange pastry 30

Crisp almond tuiles, peaches in white
    wine with 44
Crumble
    banana 24
    rhubarb, with wholewheat
      ginger topping 53
Custard apple 11

Date 8-9
Deep-dish blackberry and apple
    pie 26

Eve's pudding with a lemon
    topping 16
Exotic fruit salad 32

Fig 9
Fool, gooseberry, with pistachio nuts
    and crystallized rose petals 34
Fresh orange salad with honey and
    orange flower water 40
Fritters, apple 17
Fruit salad
    exotic 32
    winter 60

Ginger ice cream, melon filled
    with 38

Gooseberry 9
    fool with pistachio nuts and
      crystallized rose petals 34
Granadilla 11
Grape 9
    sponge with apricot glaze 35
Grapefruit 9
    grilled 9
Greengage 9

Ice cream
    apple and honey with blackberry
      sauce 18
    melon filled with ginger 38
    raspberry 51

Kiwi fruit 9
    and lime cheesecake 36

Lemon 9
    topping, Eve's pudding with 16
Lime 10
    cheesecake, kiwi fruit and 36
Loganberry 10
Lychee 10

Mandarin 13
Mango 10

Melon 10-11
   filled with ginger ice cream 38
Muesli, apple, with honey and
   almonds 20

Nectarine 11

Open apple tart 22
Orange 11
   salad, fresh, with honey and
     orange flower water 40
   water ice served in orange skins 41

Papaya 11
Passion fruit 11
Pawpaw 11
Peach(es) 11
   brulée 42
   cardinal 43
   in white wine with crisp almond
     tuiles 44
Pear(s) 11
   belle Hélène 45
   in red wine 48
   tart with chocolate pastry 46
Persimmon 12
Pies
   bilberry plate 25

deep-dish blackberry and
   apple 26
Pineapple 12
   sorbet 49
Plate pie, bilberry 25
Plum 12
   meringue 49
Poaching 5-6
Pomegranate 12
Preparation and cooking of fruit 5-6
Pudding, summer 58

Quince 12

Raspberry 12
   ice cream 51
   and redcurrant tart 52
Redcurrant 12
   tart, raspberry and 52
Red wine, pears in 48
Rhubarb 13
   crumble with wholewheat ginger
     topping 53
Rødgrød 54

Satsuma 13
Sorbet
   blackcurrant with cassis 29

63

pineapple 49
Sponge, grape, with apricot glaze 35
Strawberry(ies) 13
    with coeurs à la crème 57
    tartlets 55
Summer pudding 58

Tangerine 13
Tartlets, strawberry 55
Tarts
    cranberry lattice with orange
        pastry 30

open apple 22
pear, with chocolate pastry 46
raspberry and redcurrant 52

Water ice, orange, served in orange
    skins 41
White wine, peaches in, with crisp
    almond tuiles 44
Winter fruit salad 60